IN PURSUIT OF GREAT FOOD

A Plant-Based Shopping Guide

OF WASHINGTON

Vegan Publishers™

Published by:
Vegan Publishers, Danvers, MA, www.veganpublishers.com

Cover and text design: Nicola May Design

Printed in the United States of America

ISBN: 978-1-940184-21-0

Table of Contents

Acknowledgements

In writing this book, we're grateful to the following people who gave us advice and support on the way: Brandee Hawkins, Rachel Huff-Wagenborg, Jinda Chaijinda, Sarah Montague, Cheryl Redmond, Susan Rose, Emma Strombom, Eric Vanderwall, and all those at Vegan Publishers who helped make this book happen.

CHAPTER 1

INTRODUCTION

Shopping is a vital link in the chain for those who follow a plant-based diet, or for those who are curious and want to give it a try. The grocery store is where you'll find alternative products and new ingredients to purchase and enjoy. We've put together this practical guide to help you learn about the many different plant-based choices to buy, and how to get the best value in time and money from your food budget.

Many people are on a tight budget and worry that eating healthy, plant-based food will be expensive. However, if you are willing to plan and prepare your own meals from basic ingredients, you can save quite a bit of money. For those who often find themselves short on time, there's a wide selection of convenience and prepared products to choose from.

Before going further, let's just make sure you know what we mean when we use the terms "plant-based," "vegan," or "vegetarian" when referring to diets:

> *A plant-based diet is a diet based on plant foods, such as fruits, vegetables, whole grains, and legumes, and includes no foods derived from animals. This is also called a total vegetarian or vegan diet. Among the different varieties of vegan diets, those that are high in fiber and lowest in fat, sugar, and salt (HiFi LoFaSS) are the healthiest.*

A vegetarian diet is a diet free of meat, poultry, and fish.
Total vegetarian or vegan diets are a subset of this group.
Lacto-ovo vegetarian diets include dairy and eggs.

A diet totally free of any animal products is the best for your health, for the environment, and for the animals. However, every step you take that replaces an animal product with a plant-based food gives you, the planet, and all who share it with us a bit of benefit.

Following a plant-based diet is popular these days, and for many good reasons. The food we choose to eat is usually the single most important factor affecting our health. Physician and author Joel Fuhrman, analyzing a study of Californian vegetarians, said, "When we look at the subset who had followed a vegetarian diet for at least half their life, it appears they lived about 13 years longer."[1] This is because their rates of heart disease, certain forms of cancer, stroke, and diabetes—to name just a few diseases—are reduced dramatically by giving up animal products. Numerous medical studies have shown that a plant-based diet not only helps prevent these diseases but also forms a valuable part of treatment for those already struggling with many such chronic conditions and may actually help reverse them.

A plant-based diet is not just a solution to our health problems. The production of meat, especially in intensive "factory" farms where large numbers of animals are kept in close confinement, is very damaging to the environment. According to Richard Oppenlander in his book *Comfortably Unaware*, manure runoff causes serious water pollution, and livestock rearing is the main cause of rainforest destruction. A 2009 Worldwatch Institute report stated that meat production is also the biggest generator of greenhouse gases, worsening the global warming problem.

Global hunger is a problem that worries many people. There are over 60 billion farm animals raised each year, and those animals consume huge quantities of crops that could have been made available to hungry people. According to James McWilliams, in his book *Just Food*, it takes at least sixteen pounds of grain to produce a pound of beef, whereas each pound of grain could be fed directly to humans—as bread,

---

1. Joel Fuhrman, *Eat to Live* (New York: Little, Brown and Company, 2011).

for example.[2] Professor David Pimentel, writing in the *Cornell Chronicle* in 1997, said, "If all the grain currently fed to livestock in the United States were consumed directly by people, the number of people who could be fed would be nearly 800 million."[3] That means that we'd have enough food to feed the entirety of the world's hungry people. While global hunger is a complicated issue, it is increasingly difficult to feed a growing population on the limited agricultural land that is available. People in developing countries choosing to eat more animal products as they become attracted to a Western lifestyle only makes the problem worse.

Of course, we should also remember that every plant-based meal saves farm animals from hardship. Factory farms are designed to produce meat efficiently and cheaply, without caring about the conditions of the animals, and even grass-fed or free-range animals are ultimately slaughtered. Many people want to feel good knowing that animals weren't harmed to produce their food. Paul McCartney has said that if slaughterhouses had glass walls, everyone would be a vegetarian!

The food we bless at the dinner table has always been a primary concern of every faith and tradition. You can be assured that all the major religions allow a plant-based diet as an option, and many widely respected religious leaders have been vegetarian, or have advocated the desirability of a vegetarian diet.

And so, for the sake of your health, the environment, the animals, the hungry people of the world, and as nourishment for your spirit, you can see why a plant-based diet is a wise choice. But it's also a delicious choice. Switching over to a vegan diet, or even just including more plant-based foods in your meal, is an adventure that is both interesting and fun. Trying new foods and learning as you go will give you a chance to be creative.

We recommend two books you might find helpful if you want to learn more. *Say No to Meat: the 411 on Ditching Meat and Going Veg*, by Amanda Strombom and Stewart Rose, has lots of helpful information on "the why and how" of a plant-based diet written in an easy question and answer format, and includes some easy but tasty starter recipes. *Eat Vegan on $4 a Day*, by Ellen Jaffe Jones, is packed full of money saving recipes.

---

2. James E. McWilliams, *Just Food* (New York: Back Bay Books, 2010) 125.
3. "U.S. could feed 800 million people with grain that livestock eat, Cornell ecologist advises animal scientists," *Cornell Chronicle*, August 7, 1997, http://www.news.cornell.edu/stories/1997/08/us-could-feed-800-million-people-grain-livestock-eat

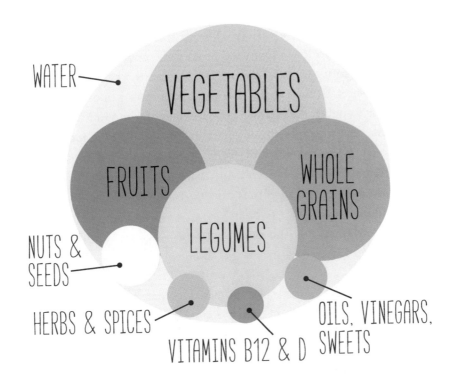

WATER

VEGETABLES

FRUITS

WHOLE GRAINS

NUTS & SEEDS

LEGUMES

HERBS & SPICES

VITAMINS B12 & D

OILS, VINEGARS, SWEETS

CHAPTER 2

—THE HEALTHY PLANT-BASED DIET—

The Plant-Based Food Bowl shown above represents the foods you should include in your diet and the relative priorities of each group. Plan your main meals around vegetables, whole grains, fruits, legumes, and nuts. Fruit is great for breakfast, desserts, and snacks. Use herbs and spices for flavoring, with modest amounts of salt and sugar if desired. Use plant-based oils, but no more than necessary.

For drinks, water, tea, coffee, and plant-based milks such as soy or almond milk are the healthiest choices. Go easy on drinks with added sweeteners and fruit juices, since they are usually high in sugar. If you enjoy carbonated drinks, choose sodas sweetened with herbal extracts, or naturally flavored seltzer water.

As long as you eat a variety of foods from each of these groups, you don't need to worry about getting enough protein. If you're eating a sufficient quantity of good quality food to get the calories you need, you will also get all the protein you need, and in fact, most Americans following a Standard American Diet (SAD) get far too much protein.

While many people think they need to drink milk for calcium, you can get plenty of calcium from green leafy vegetables such as collard greens, bok choy, broccoli, and many other plant foods. Fortified plant-milks and orange juice, plus calcium-set tofu, are also good sources of calcium.

You'll also get all the other nutrients you need, with just two possible exceptions:

- **Vitamin B12** is made by a soil-based bacteria and accumulates in animals as they eat food from the ground. Since we wash or peel our plant foods, supplementation is needed if you're not eating any animal products. A one-a-day type of vitamin tablet gives you plenty of B12.
- **Vitamin D** is made by sunlight's action on the skin. Since many people spend most of their time indoors, and cover up with clothing and sunscreen when outside, supplementation is recommended for most people, especially if you live in a northern latitude where the sunshine is limited to begin with!

Here's a quick list of some important nutrients and some of the best sources:

- **Calcium** – almonds, bok choy, broccoli, cabbage, collard greens, fortified orange juice
- **Folate (folic acid)** – leafy green vegetables, whole grain wheat, many legumes
- **Iodine** – sea salt, ordinary iodized salt, seaweed such as kelp
- **Iron** – beans, broccoli, collard greens, red lentils, kale, watermelon, whole grains (consume with vitamin C-containing foods to maximize iron absorption)
- **Omega-3 fatty acids** – walnuts, soy, flax and chia seeds, oils such as flax oil or canola oil

- **Protein** – beans, lentils, peas, soy products, nuts, quinoa, and whole grains
- **Vitamin A** (in the form of beta-carotene) – carrots, butternut squash, pumpkin, sweet potatoes
- **Vitamin B1** (thiamine) – barley, brazil nuts, lentils, nutritional yeast, oatmeal, peas, sunflower seeds, wheat germ
- **Vitamin B2** (riboflavin) – almonds, leafy greens, legumes, mushrooms
- **Vitamin B3** (niacin) – barley, mushrooms, peas, tempeh, whole grain wheat
- **Vitamin B5** (pantothenic acid) – very widely available in most plant foods
- **Vitamin B6** (pyridoxine) – bananas, figs, garbanzo beans, potatoes, soybeans, whole grains
- **Vitamin B7** (biotin) – our bodies make more than we need
- **Vitamin B12** – enriched foods or supplements
- **Vitamin C** – most fresh fruit, especially citrus fruits, and most vegetables
- **Vitamin D** – sunshine on skin, enriched plant-based milks, supplements
- **Vitamin E** – almonds, asparagus, broccoli, hazelnuts, pumpkin, spinach, wheat germ
- **Zinc** – tofu, tempeh, garbanzo beans, lentils, oatmeal, cashews, peanuts

Fiber is widely available throughout the plant kingdom. Insoluble fiber attracts water and makes stools bulky and soft, so it helps move waste products through the colon quickly. Soluble fiber dissolves in water, encourages the growth of beneficial bacteria in the bowel, and helps eliminate cholesterol. Neither kind is absorbed by the body. Most plant foods contain a mixture of both soluble and insoluble fiber in varying proportions. A particularly good source of insoluble fiber is wheat bran, while oatmeal and bananas are good sources of soluble fiber. Animal foods have no fiber.

Probiotics are beneficial live bacteria either naturally present in fermented products, such as yogurt, miso, sauerkraut, or tempeh, or added during production. They are thought to promote healthy bacteria in the intestine. **Prebiotics** are natural substances that reliably pass through to the intestines, where they specifically nourish the good bacteria. Some examples of prebiotics that may be added to food products are inulin, from chicory root, and fructo-oligosaccarides (FOS), which occur naturally in artichoke, asparagus, garlic, and onions.

Phytonutrients are nutrients from plants and are not commonly included in lists of important vitamins and minerals. There are many different phytonutrients; new ones are being discovered all the time. Here are just a few better known ones:

- Anthocyanins in blueberries
- Beta carotene in carrots
- Catechin in tea
- Genistein in soy
- Lutein and xeaxanthin in corn and summer squash
- Lycopene in tomatoes, especially in cooked tomato sauce
- Sulfarophane in broccoli
- Sulfides and thiols in garlic and onion

They have been found to provide a wide variety of health benefits, including anticancer, anti-inflammatory, and antioxidant effects, and are some of the components that go into making up the plant-based diet health advantage. Eat a wide range of plant foods to get as many different phytonutrients as you can.

Plants may also contain small amounts of pesticides and herbicides, which could be damaging to our health. We therefore recommend purchasing **organic foods** whenever they are available and affordable. They are better both for you and the planet. However, far more pesticides and herbicides concentrate in animal tissues during the life of the animal, leading to a much higher level of these toxic substances in animal foods than in plant foods, so just by going vegan you'll avoid most of them. Organics take you the rest of the way. (See page 51 for an explanation of organic certification and page 63 for a list of the Dirty Dozen™—produce that contains the most pesticides and herbicides.)

CHAPTER 3

—THE PLANT-BASED KITCHEN—

Preparing meals that are both healthy and delicious is easy if you have the right ingredients on hand. Choose foods that give you a lot of bang for your culinary buck, foods that offer great flavor, great nutrition, and if possible, convenience too. Take quinoa (pronounced "keen-wah"), for example: an ancient grain with an appealing, lightly fluffy texture that has an excellent protein profile, vitamins and minerals, and is quick and easy to cook. Read on for more ingredients that deserve a place in your healthy kitchen.

3.1 Legumes, Beans, Nuts, and Seeds

Beans and Lentils

Beans are tiny bundles of nutrition, providing complex carbohydrates, protein, fiber, vitamins, and minerals. Dried beans are the most economical and aren't difficult to cook; they just require a little planning ahead. When buying dried beans, shop at a store with high turnover, and look for beans that are plump and smooth, not shriveled. Canned beans make a quicker, more convenient alternative and will work fine in most recipes that call for dried. Organic brands are often lower in sodium than conventional brands. Be sure to check the ingredient label.

Here are some common bean varieties:

- **Adzuki** (also spelled azuki or aduki) beans, are small, dark reddish-brown beans with a mild, sweet flavor, used in Japanese cooking.
- **Black beans**, or turtle beans, are used in Latin American and Caribbean cooking and go particularly well with spicy foods and citrus flavors.
- **Black-eyed peas**, or cowpeas, are popular in Southern cuisine. They contribute their mild, earthy flavor to the dish called Hoppin' John.
- **Chickpeas**, or garbanzo beans, are used in Mediterranean and Indian cooking. Firm and slightly nutty in flavor, they're great in soups, salads, and indispensable for hummus.
- **Kidney beans** are robust and meaty, and can hold their own in dishes like red beans and rice. A type of French kidney bean, called the flageolet, has a delicate green color and is mild and tender.
- **Lima beans**, or butter beans, are large, pale green beans, most famously paired with corn to make succotash.
- **Pinto beans**, with their pink and brown markings and hearty flavor, are used in refried beans. They work well in chili and other stews.
- **Great northern beans**, navy beans (also called Yankee beans), and cannellini are all mild-tasting white beans and are good in soups. Large great northern beans and small navy beans are both used for baked beans.
- **Lentils** are the easiest legumes to digest, making them a good choice for beginners. Although canned lentils are available, dried lentils cook quickly and don't need to be presoaked, making them suitable for weeknight dinners. Varieties include common brown-green lentils, also known just as green lentils; French green lentils, also called lentilles de Puy; beluga lentils, which are small and black; and red lentils, which cook quickly, becoming soft and golden.
- **Dal** is the Indian name for peas, beans, and lentils that have been split and sometimes skinned; they're sold in Indian markets. Varieties include chana dal (from a relative of the chickpea),

masoor dal (from pink lentils), moong dal (from mung beans), toor dal (from yellow lentils), and urad dal (from black lentils, although the dal is white because the lentils have been skinned).

Some people worry about experiencing intestinal issues such as excessive gas after consuming beans. If you're new to this way of eating, we recommend you start with lentils, the easiest legumes to digest, and gradually include small quantities of other beans in your diet. If you're preparing dried beans, a small amount of ordinary baking soda (one-fourth teaspoon per gallon of water) added to the soaking water will very significantly reduce raffinose and stachyose, the gas-causing sugars naturally present in varying amounts in beans. Rinse canned beans thoroughly in a colander or sieve before use to help remove these sugars.

Soyfoods

Soyfoods are valued not only for their high protein content, with generous amounts of all the essential amino acids, but also for their phytonutrients (health-promoting substances in plant foods in addition to vitamins, minerals, and fiber), which have many health benefits. You can find myriad soy-containing products on the market. Meat analogues like veggie burgers and dogs offer convenience and occasional social advantages, such as having a veggie roast at Thanksgiving. For even greater health benefit and more versatility in the kitchen, choose traditional, minimally processed soyfoods, such as tofu and tempeh. Here are the most common soy products:

- **Edamame** are green soybeans. You can buy them fresh or frozen, in the pod or out. In their pods, they make a wonderful snack or appetizer, steamed and sprinkled with coarse salt. Use your teeth to pull the beans from their pods. Shelled edamame are a tasty addition to soups and stand in for lima beans in dishes like succotash. Edamame are fun to grow; if you have a garden, consider planting a row or two of these protein-filled legumes.
- **Miso** is a fermented soy product that has a savory quality (called umami) that provides depth of flavor to soups, sauces, and dress-

ings. It's also a rich source of phytonutrients. Miso is primarily made of soy but may include barley, chickpeas, or rice. The color and flavor of miso depend on its ingredients and fermentation time. Generally speaking, dark misos have been aged longer and have a more assertive, saltier taste than lighter ones. Some miso is very salty, so add a little at a time, tasting as you go. If you're using unpasteurized miso in soups or stews, add it at the beginning of cooking to ensure it is cooked thoroughly.

- **Tempeh** has a chewy texture and a hearty, somewhat nutty flavor. It's well worth your time making friends with this nutritional superstar. One serving packs twenty grams of protein, six grams of fiber, and plenty of health-promoting phytonutrients; plus it's low in fat. Tempeh is made from soybeans that have been cooked and fermented with a special culture that binds the beans together into a firm, sliceable patty. The fermentation process also makes tempeh easy to digest. Tempeh easily absorbs flavors and can be baked, boiled, crumbled, fried, or steamed.

- **Tofu's** smooth texture and mild flavor makes it a kitchen chameleon, able to transform itself into main dishes as well as desserts. Some brands of tofu use calcium in their production so are a good source of calcium as well as protein. There are two basic types: regular and silken. Regular tofu may be labeled soft, firm, or extra firm, with softer tofu more suitable for steaming and firmer more suitable for frying. You can also buy low-fat, preflavored, baked, or smoked tofu. Silken tofu is most suitable for desserts and smoothies where a creamy texture is required. Firmness varies from soft to extra firm, however, so you may need to experiment. Tofu is available in refrigerated or aseptic packaging. Whatever kind you buy, once you open the package, cover any unused tofu with water and refrigerate it until needed.

- **Soymilk** comes in a variety of flavors, but to replace cow's milk in recipes like quiche or mashed potatoes, stick to the plain, unsweetened kind. Most brands of soymilk are enriched with calcium and other nutrients and have an amino content similar to milk. Like milk, soymilk will curdle; adding one tablespoon of lemon juice or vinegar to a cup of soymilk will make a buttermilk substitute. Just like milk, soymilk can spoil; keep refrigerated cartons and opened aseptic cartons refrigerated, and use open cartons within a week. (See page 38 for a description of other nondairy milks)

- **Soy sauce** is a brew of fermented soybeans and roasted wheat, with water and salt added. It can range from light and thin (not to be confused with low-sodium) to dark and thick. Thai thin soy sauce is an example of the former style, while Chinese black sweet soy sauce is an example of the latter. Shoyu is the Japanese word for soy sauce. Tamari is Japanese soy sauce that has been brewed without wheat. It is slightly thicker and richer tasting than regular soy sauce. The best soy sauce is aged and contains no additives. Soy sauce is salty; one tablespoon provides more than a third of your daily value for sodium, so use it sparingly. "Lite" or low-sodium soy sauce has roughly half the sodium of regular soy sauce. Bragg Liquid Aminos is made from unfermented soybeans. It has slightly less sodium than regular soy sauce and may be used as a substitute.

Peanuts

While commonly thought of as a nut, peanuts are actually legumes and share many of their nutritional characteristics. You can find peanuts sold whole in their shells, in packets of mixed nuts, or by themselves. Avoid peanuts fried in oil and covered in salt—dry-roasted, unsalted peanuts are best. Peanut butter is a popular spread for all ages. Choose brands where the only ingredient is peanuts.

Nuts and Seeds

Good news for nut lovers: nuts do more than add texture and flavor to meatless meals such as salads, veggie burgers, and pilafs—they also add nutrients. Nuts have protein, vitamins, minerals, and fiber. They also have an excellent array of phytonutrients, and some are very high in omega-3 essential fatty acids. Nuts have been shown to lower the risk of many common diseases such as cardiovascular disease.

Here are a few of our favorite nuts:

- **Chestnuts** are actually low in calories and contain some very special probiotics.
- **Hazelnuts** have high levels of phytonutrients, especially if the skin is eaten with the nut.
- **Pistachios** are a good choice for those looking for extra fiber as they contain as much fiber as oatmeal.
- **Walnuts** are an excellent source of omega-3 essential fatty acids. Just one ounce of walnuts contains a full day's requirement.
- **Cashews** are a good source for zinc, one of the harder to find minerals.
- **Almonds** are a good choice for vitamin E and calcium.

A little goes a long way when it comes to nuts. A one-ounce serving, five to seven times a week, is all that is needed to reap several health benefits. Beware of nut spoilers! Many nuts are sold fried in oil and heavily salted. This is a shame because it spoils, to some extent, the health value of nuts and overshadows their desirable, natural, nutty taste. Instead choose dry-roasted, unsalted nuts. When shopping, buy whole nuts and chop them yourself as needed; small chopped pieces are more vulnerable to oxidation (exposure to air, which can make them stale). Store nuts in a cool place to help keep them fresh.

When considering the crunch factor, don't forget about seeds. Chia seeds and flaxseeds are excellent choices for omega-3 essential fatty acids. Hemp seeds are a good choice for fiber, omega-3s, and protein. Sesame seeds are a good choice for those looking for some extra calcium in their diet. Pumpkin seeds have a generous amount of zinc.

Just as with nuts, a few seeds go a long way. They need only be eaten in moderation for the best health benefit. Beware of seeds fried in oil and then salted. Look for dry-roasted, unsalted, whole seeds for both best flavor and health. For storage and best shelf life, keep them refrigerated, and only chop or grind seeds just before you use them.

3.2 Whole Grains and Whole-Grain Products

There's no denying the nutritional benefit—or the satisfying taste—of whole grains, which are rich with vitamins, minerals, and fiber. Much of the nutritional value of whole grains is lost when they are refined. In refined grains, the important parts of the grain that contain much of the valuable nutrients are taken out, so they're no longer "whole grains." So-called "enriched" wheat and flour only have some of the nutrients replaced.

If you can shop in a store with a bulk aisle, this is a good place to shop for whole grains and will save you some money over prepackaged products. Shop at a market that has rapid turnover for the freshest grains, buy only as much as you can use in a month or two, and store away from heat and light.

Corn is available in whole-grain form as corn on the cob and frozen niblets. It can also be "air popped" to make healthy, whole-grain popcorn. Corn is actually quite nutritious, but sadly it is often drenched in butter and salt—a shame, since doing so not only reduces its health advantages but also hides its naturally delicious flavor.

Oats are roasted after being harvested and cleaned, which helps give them their distinctive flavor. They are then hulled, but this doesn't remove all the bran and germ, so they keep much of their nutritional value. They are processed by steaming and rolling (rolled oats), slicing thinly (steel-cut oats), partially cooking (instant oats), or grinding (oat flour) to give them the consistency and cooking time required. Oats are an excellent source of soluble fiber and minerals. They make a great choice for breakfast, but try to find the least processed oats with few added ingredients, as many commercial oat cereals contain added sugars, flavorings, and even colors, which have no nutritional value.

Rice: All the types of rice listed below are available in whole-grain form. In general, whole-grain rice takes twice as long to cook as its white counterparts, although quick-cooking brown rice is available. Here are some less familiar varieties of rice definitely worth trying:

- **Arborio** is a short-grain rice native to Italy and used in risotto. Because of the composition of its starches, Arborio turns creamy-soft on the outside while retaining a firm interior.

- **Basmati** is a long-grain rice used in Indian and South Asian cooking. It cooks up fluffy and separate because it has been aged to decrease its moisture content. Basmati has a delicately nutty, almost popcorn-like aroma and flavor.
- **Jasmine** is a long-grain rice with a lightly perfumed aroma and flavor, produced in Thailand and used in Asian cooking and as a substitute for basmati rice.
- **Sticky rice** is also called glutinous or sweet rice. This short-grain rice is used for sushi and desserts. Like all rice, it doesn't contain gluten, despite its name!
- **Wild rice** is not actually a rice but comes from an entirely different crop and was a favorite of American Indians. It may be either truly wild or cultivated. Wild rice requires a long cooking time but has a wonderful texture and flavor that is good alone or in combination with other rice or grains.

Other varieties of rice include Bhutanese red, black Japonica, black forbidden, Himalayan red, and Wehani. Each of these is a whole-grain rice with its own distinct color, flavor, and texture.

Spelt and kamut are ancient forms of wheat that were the forerunners of the triticale wheat grown today. They cook up the same, but many people find them (especially spelt) easier to digest. These two grains have developed quite the following in recent years, and some people with mild gluten issues seem to tolerate spelt just fine. See page 28 for other options for those with gluten sensitivities.

Whole-grain wheat comes from the crop in little oval shaped objects called berries. Wheat berries (triticale) are especially nutritious. They cook up much the same as any hot cereal.

In addition to the familiar grains listed above, here are just a few standouts among the many excellent grain choices available:

- **Amaranth**, not technically a grain but a seed, is a good source of vitamin B6, iron, and zinc. Nutty-tasting amaranth makes good porridge, and the little seeds work well blended with other grains.
- **Barley** is sold as whole grains that have been hulled or pearled. Hulled barley has had only the outer husk removed, leaving the

nutritious bran layer intact. Pearl barley has had the bran layer polished off as well, so it's somewhat less nutritious, though also faster cooking, than hulled barley. Barley may have been the first ever cultivated grain in ancient times.

- **Buckwheat**, despite its name, is not wheat but a member of an entirely different family of plants. It's also known as kasha. It is gluten-free, nutritious, and versatile. It can be quickly cooked for a hot cereal, and also comes in pasta form.
- **Millet** is sold hulled and cooks up fluffy with a mild flavor. Millet is native to Africa and Asia and is a delicious alternative grain.
- **Quinoa**, not technically a grain but a seed, is native to the Andes and offers excellent nutrition, with a near perfect protein profile of amino acids. Better yet, it has an appealing, nutty taste and a delicately crunchy texture; it cooks quickly; and it works in everything from hot breakfast cereal to pilaf. When picked, quinoa has a protective coating of soapy-tasting saponins. Some quinoa sold in this country has been prewashed to remove this layer, but it's a good idea to rinse quinoa before using it.
- **Teff**, whose name means "lost," is originally from Ethiopia and is an extremely tiny grain, usually sold as a whole grain. Teff is particularly high in protein and calcium. Its size makes it suitable as a hot breakfast cereal, and in Africa, it is also used to make a spongy bread called injera.
- **Wheat germ** is the innermost portion of the wheat berry. Its nutty flavor and concentrated nutrients make a perfect addition to cookies, cakes, and breads, both in the batter and sprinkled on top. It's a great addition to both hot and cold cereals, and tastes great as a topping for frozen nondairy desserts. Wheat germ sold in bottles must be refrigerated after opening. Fresh wheat germ, sold in bags, must be refrigerated even before opening.

Pasta and Noodles

With a jar of tomato sauce and a box of pasta in your pantry, you're never more than minutes away from a satisfying meal. Pasta is sold fresh in the refrigerated section or in shelf-stable packages, and comes in a wide variety of shapes and sizes. Pasta is usually made from a type of wheat flour called durum semolina. If you choose dried pasta made with whole-wheat flour, you'll get a nutritional boost from the extra fiber (note that some varieties of pasta contain egg ingredients).

These days you'll also find pasta made from other grains such as spelt, rice, buckwheat, quinoa, corn, and others. Be sure not to overcook these pastas; their lower gluten content means they're apt to fall apart unless served al dente (still slightly firm).

In addition to the traditional Italian-style pastas, Asian noodles provide a range of textures and flavors that can dramatically expand your cooking repertoire. Here are a few popular choices:

- **Bean threads**, also known as cellophane noodles, glass noodles, or woon sen, are made from mung bean starch and become translucent when cooked. They are used in soups, salads, and stir-fries and have a somewhat gelatinous texture.
- **Ramen noodles** are wheat noodles that are often fried before being dried. Ramen comes in various shapes and lengths. It may be thick, thin, or even ribbonlike, as well as straight or wrinkled.
- **Rice noodles** come in different widths, from rice vermicelli (very thin and threadlike) to wide. Also called rice sticks, ban pho, or sen lek, they're used in Chinese, Vietnamese, Malaysian, and Thai cooking. Thinner noodles are used for soups or as spring roll fillings, and thicker ones are used in stir-fries.
- **Soba noodles**, or Japanese buckwheat noodles, have a chewy texture and hearty flavor. Flat like fettuccine, they come in different widths.
- **Somen noodles** are thin Japanese wheat noodles, usually served cold.
- **Udon noodles** are thick Japanese wheat noodles, usually served in soups.

Flours

If you like to bake, there are plenty of ways to boost the nutrition of your baked goods, starting with the flour and sugar. Whole-wheat flour is made from the entire kernel of wheat—bran, germ, and all. It has more fiber, vitamins, and minerals than white flour but also produces coarser, denser baked goods, so you may want to replace just a portion of the all-purpose flour in a recipe with whole-wheat flour. There are three basic kinds:

- **Regular whole-wheat flour** is milled from hard, or high-protein, wheat and is best suited for yeast breads, where it contributes a hearty texture and robust flavor.
- **Whole-wheat pastry flour** is milled from a soft, or low-protein, variety of wheat that doesn't form much gluten (strong elastic strands of protein) when it's mixed. It's best for cakes, cookies, pies, and quick breads, where lightness and tenderness are more desirable than strength and elasticity.
- **White whole-wheat flour** is milled from a variety of light-colored wheat that gives it a pale color and mild flavor. It has the same protein content as regular whole-wheat flour and is used the same way.

For those with wheat or gluten sensitivities, or who want to introduce different flavors, textures, and nutrients to their baked goods, you have many other flours from which to choose. These include buckwheat, corn, potato, quinoa, and rice flour, which contain no gluten. Barley, rye, and spelt flour do contain gluten or gluten-like substances, and oat flour can be contaminated with gluten, but these can be tolerated by some with mild gluten sensitivities. Low- to no-gluten flours may be blended with all-purpose flour or used by themselves in desserts that don't rely on gluten for structure, such as fruit crisps.

Store all whole-wheat flours, including wheat germ, in a cool, dry place to keep them fresh.

3.3 Fruits and Vegetables

You've probably heard it many times: try to eat between five and nine servings of fruits and vegetables (or even more) every day, and choose them from all the colors of the rainbow. The numbers may sound high, but it's really not that hard to achieve. In most cases, a serving is between one-half cup (for berries and chopped fruit and vegetables) and one cup (for raw leafy greens). As for the rainbow part, shopping for color adds more than just visual appeal to your plate. The same substances that make brightly colored vegetables and fruits so attractive are also responsible for much of their healthfulness. These nutrients, called phytonutrients, help prevent a variety of diseases.

The fresher the fruit or vegetable (unless frozen), the more of its important nutrients are intact, so shop for seasonal produce. Tropical fruit, while not local for many of us, is still a worthwhile choice.

Consider buying organic, at least for heavily sprayed produce such as strawberries and spinach (see the Dirty Dozen™ list on page 63). Look for fruits and vegetables that feel heavy for their size and have taut, shiny skin. Leaves should be brightly colored, not yellowed or washed out. Root vegetables should be firm, not flabby or mushy.

Finally, eat a wide variety of fruits and vegetables, cooked or raw. You'll get a more interesting array of tastes and textures, and better nutrition, too.

Below is just a sampling of nutritional stars among the huge variety of fruits and vegetables you can choose from, listed with their notable nutrients. The next time you're in the produce aisle, why not pick up a few?

Fruits

Berries – Bright, jewel-toned berries are priceless sources of phytonutrients. Blueberries, for instance, have the highest level of certain phytonutrients of any fruit or vegetable. Blackberries offer vitamins C and E and are a good source of fiber. Enjoy berries fresh in the summer, and freeze them or buy them frozen for use in desserts or smoothies at other times of year.

Melons – All provide a good source of potassium and vitamin C, and orange-fleshed varieties like cantaloupe and crenshaw have exceptional amounts of beta-carotene, which your body converts to vitamin A. Perhaps the star of the melon family is watermelon; in addition to the above nutrients, it offers iron and a healthy dose of lycopene, a phytonutrient that has powerful anticancer properties. A slice of fresh melon is delicious as an appetizer, as part of a fresh fruit salad, or as an anytime snack.

Tree Fruits – Tree fruits make convenient, portable snacks as well as delicious desserts. Apples are rich in pectin, a type of soluble fiber. Pears are even more nutritious than apples. Eat them unpeeled, as their skins contain valuable nutrients too. Apricots, fresh or dried, are high in beta-carotene and provide potassium and fiber. Cherries contain phytonutrients that may help fight disease.

Tropical Fruits – Most tropical fruits are high in potassium and fiber, beta-carotene, and vitamin C. One orange provides your day's requirement of vitamin C, and a mango gives you a day's worth of beta-carotene. Avocados, with their mild flavor and high content of healthy monounsaturated fat, make a great alternative to butter or margarine for spreading on toast. Pink and red grapefruits contain pectin. Half a grapefruit, chilled, forms an ideal part of your breakfast, as does a banana, which contains high levels of potassium and pectin.

Other Fruits – Grapes, especially red and purple ones, contain potent phytonutrients. Most of these nutrients are concentrated in the skin. Children love grapes as a healthy snack that is easy to eat. Raisins are a convenient alternative to grapes, although some nutrients are lost by being dried, and the natural sugars are more concentrated.

Vegetables

Cruciferous Vegetables – The large family of cruciferous vegetables includes those that form heads, like broccoli, brussels sprouts, cabbage, and cauliflower, and leafy vegetables like bok choy, chard, kale, collard, and mustard greens. All contain sulfur-containing phytonutrients that have significant anticancer properties. They are also good sources of beta-carotene (which your body converts to vitamin A), folate, calcium, and potassium. These vegetables are best steamed, microwaved, or chopped into small pieces in a stir-fry or other cooked dish. Many people add raw leafy vegetables such as kale to a smoothie for extra nutrition.

Salad Vegetables – Most lettuces are modest in the nutrition department, although darker-leaved lettuces contain more nutrients than those with pale leaves. Note that the common iceberg lettuce has the least nutrition of all lettuces, whereas romaine lettuce is more nutritious.

However, many leafy greens used for salad are part of the large family of cruciferous vegetables; as such, they provide a fair amount of nutrients, including calcium, folate, beta-carotene, and vitamin C. Eating mesclun mix or spring mix (sold loose or prepackaged) is an easy way to get many of these greens at once; they consist of an assortment of baby cruciferous greens, such as arugula, chard, mizuna, and tatsoi. These leafy vegetables are usually eaten raw in a salad, but some, like spinach, are great when lightly steamed.

Root Vegetables – Root vegetables add heartiness and a satisfying stick-to-the-ribs quality to meals. Beets, carrots, and parsnips are rich in anticancer properties and minerals. They can be steamed, baked, or roasted. Onions (and their relatives leeks, scallions, and shallots) contain valuable phytonutrients. They are usually chopped and included in stir-fries and casseroles. Sweet potatoes—baked, mashed, or roasted—are a nutritional trade-up from white potatoes.

Squashes – Zucchini squash supplies very important phytonutrients that help prevent the eye disease macular degeneration. Summer squashes such as zucchini or pattypan squash can be eaten cooked or raw. Winter squashes include acorn, buttercup, butternut, delicata, spaghetti, hubbard, kabocha, and pumpkin. The common butternut squash is a very good source of dietary fiber. Squash is usually baked but can also be steamed. Most need to be peeled before or after cooking, but the skin of delicata squash is soft enough to eat. Plain canned pumpkin is very healthy and also convenient for adding to soups, baked goods, and desserts.

Other Vegetables – Mushrooms are more nutritious than you might think. They contain B vitamins, copper, selenium, potassium, and some, such as shiitake, are being studied for their anticancer properties. They are tasty raw in salads and add a delicious flavor to stews and gravy. A large portobello mushroom, marinated in a balsamic vinegar dressing and grilled, makes an excellent substitute for a hamburger on a bun.

Peppers, especially red and orange, are rich in beta-carotene and vitamins. They can be eaten raw in salads, baked, or stir-fried. Tomatoes are a good source of vitamin C. They're also rich in lycopene; cooking makes this cancer-fighting nutrient more absorbable, as does serving the tomatoes as a tomato sauce.

There are many other vegetables to explore, with various health benefits to each. Feel free to experiment with any vegetables and enjoy!

3.4 Herbs and Spices

You can add big flavor to your meals with just a little chopping or a shake of a jar when you use fresh or dried herbs and spices. There is a tendency these days to make food more flavorful by just adding ever-larger amounts of sugar, salt, and fat. Herbs and spices are a better choice because they help keep the calorie count down, add more complex and satisfying flavors to food, and for those of us who eat with our noses and eyes in addition to our mouths, add a wonderful aroma and an enhanced appearance to food. Indeed, many chefs consider the herbs and spices in any dish as important as the food they complement.

Many herbs and spices also have specific health benefits. They may be anti-inflammatory, antioxidant, protective against cancer, and can even help with reducing blood pressure and cholesterol.

A huge variety of herbs and spices are available. Here are some of the most common ones you should keep in your kitchen, if you're going to be cooking regularly:

- **Basil** – Fresh basil is needed for pesto, but dried basil works well for many dishes.
- **Black pepper** – Buy whole peppercorns and grind in a pepper mill as needed.
- **Chili powder** – usually sold as a spice blend; widely used to add heat
- **Cinnamon** – a widely used spice; complements sweetness in baked goods and desserts
- **Coriander** – a spice mainly used in Indian cuisine, ground or as seeds. Fresh coriander is also known as cilantro and is widely used in Mexican cooking.
- **Cumin** – a spice used in many cuisines, ground or as seeds
- **Garlic** – used in many cuisines. Fresh garlic is best, but garlic powder can be a useful alternative.
- **Ginger** – Fresh ginger root keeps well in a plastic bag in the

freezer, and can be grated as needed. Powdered ginger can be a useful alternative.

- **Oregano** – an herb, usually used dried in Italian foods
- **Red pepper flakes** – dried flakes add heat to dishes; use sparingly
- **Rosemary** – an herb, usually used dried
- **Sage** – an herb which adds a flavor reminiscent of meat
- **Thyme** – an herb, usually used dried
- **Turmeric** – a yellow spice used in Indian cooking

Many people like to buy spice blends for convenience. Blends of spices can be useful to create a particular cuisine. For instance, Italian blend, Cajun spice, or curry powder can help produce a specific cuisine right away, so these may be a good starting point if you don't want to invest in too many different spices. In addition to being an integral part of various cuisines, spice blends are often used in meat analogues such as veggie burgers and various other faux meats. For instance, you can buy a poultry spice blend to help make a meat substitute taste like chicken. As you broaden your range of recipes, you'll find yourself gathering an ever-widening range of dried herbs and spices.

Depending on where they're grown, and how they're stored and transported, herbs and spices can sometimes be contaminated with pesticides, herbicides, industrial toxins, and bacteria. Choose organic herbs and spices, or locally grown, whenever possible to minimize this risk. Some dried herbs and spices are irradiated to kill off potential bacteria. While the FDA says that irradiated herbs are safe, cooking will destroy bacteria just as well.

To make fresh herbs last longer, remove the rubber band or twist tie holding them as soon as you get them home. If you're not planning to use them in a day or two, store fresh herbs upright in a glass of water in the refrigerator, like a bunch of flowers at the florist's. A better alternative, which will provide you with an ongoing supply, is to buy a plant for each of your favorite fresh herbs and keep them in pots on your window ledge. All fresh herbs should be thoroughly rinsed before use.

As for dried herbs and spices, remember that they have a shelf life too. Check for an expiration date. If a dried herb or spice doesn't smell like itself anymore, it's time to toss it and buy a new jar. Dried herbs should be stored in a cool, dry place out of direct sunlight. If your local food store has a bulk department, check out the bulk herb and spice section. The price is often a small percentage of what you pay for individual jars, and you can buy only the amount you need.

3.5 Sweeteners

Most sweeteners add very little nutritional value to food, so it's important to use them sparingly. However, sweeteners are valuable in adding flavor to foods, so use small quantities of natural sweeteners to enhance flavor when called for in a recipe.

Most commercial granulated sugar is processed from cane juice, using chemicals to bleach it and sometimes animal-derived charcoal ("bone char") to remove impurities, which makes it undesirable for people who wish to strictly avoid any contact with animal products. Brown sugar is not less-refined sugar, but refined sugar with molasses (a by-product of sugar manufacturing) added back in for flavor and texture.

Some products labeled as natural sugars are minimally refined and don't use bone char. Evaporated cane juice produces a sugar that is less refined, leaving more of its natural nutrients intact. These natural sugars are dark beige in color, with a sandy texture and a slight molasses flavor. They can be used cup-for-cup in place of sugar, although they don't dissolve quite as well. Evaporated fruit juice, beet sugar, and palm sugar are other alternatives.

Liquid sweeteners, such as barley malt, brown rice syrup, maple syrup, and molasses, are suitable for desserts, although they can't simply be substituted for an equal amount of granulated sugar. Generally, you would use 25 percent less liquid sweetener, and if there is liquid in the recipe, it should also be reduced by 25 percent to compensate for the added moisture provided by the sweetener. Agave syrup, made from the nectar of the agave plant, is sometimes used by vegans in place of honey. It is sweeter than honey, though not quite as thick. Also keep in mind that each liquid sweetener imparts a distinct flavor to baked goods, which is different than the neutral sweetness contributed by sugar.

Natural calorie-free, plant-derived sugar substitutes such as stevia, originally from South America, and luo han guo, originally from

Southeast Asia, have become very popular lately. They have a good safety record and a long history of traditional use. They are available in both powder and liquid form. They add sweetness without calories and can be used in place of artificial sweeteners such as aspartame, sucralose, and saccharin.

3.6 Oils and Vinegars

Many people value oils and fats for the flavor, texture, or mouthfeel they can add to food, and of course for frying. However, all fats and oils contain a lot of calories, and saturated fats from animal products stimulate the production of cholesterol and promote insulin resistance. We recommend you avoid butter and use as little oil as you can. Trans fats (partially hydrogenated oils) are even less healthy than saturated fats in some ways and should also be avoided.

Some oils are more suited for some types of cooking than others because of their varying smoke points (the temperature at which an oil begins to smoke and unhealthy compounds are formed). In general, unrefined oils—those which have not been chemically stripped of color and flavor—have lower smoke points. (For example, the smoke point of unrefined peanut oil is 320 degrees versus 440 degrees for refined peanut oil.) In addition, unrefined oils have shorter shelf lives and should be protected from heat and light during storage. Store all oils in the refrigerator after opening to minimize the risk of their going rancid.

Some other general rules of thumb:

- Oils from nuts and some seeds, such as walnut oil or flaxseed oil, are best used for salads or for baking, where they are not exposed to direct high heat.
- Sesame oil is sold in light and dark versions. The dark oil is made from roasted sesame seeds and has a stronger flavor and a low smoke point; it is best used as a flavoring in sauces or drizzled over stir-fry ingredients in the last minute of cooking.
- Any unrefined oil, including extra-virgin olive oil, is also best used in low- or no-heat dishes. Since unrefined oils tend to be more expensive, it makes sense to use them in ways that allow you to

appreciate their flavor. Olive oil not labeled extra-virgin is refined and better able to withstand higher temperatures.

- For higher-heat cooking, refined oils—those that have been processed to remove their natural flavor—such as canola, grapeseed, peanut, safflower, soybean, sunflower, and corn oil can be used. Corn and canola oil are the best choices for minimizing saturated fat content while cooking at a high heat.

Vinegar is good for more than just salad dressing—it's a low-sodium, low-calorie flavor builder that can enhance a wide range of plant-based dishes. Add zip to your meals with some of these vinegars:

- **Balsamic vinegar** is made from wine grapes that have been aged in barrels over a period of years. True balsamic vinegar is rich and syrupy—and more expensive. Supermarket balsamic-type vinegars may include red wine vinegar and caramel color but can still be tasty. Drizzle *tradizionale balsamic* (the real thing) over strawberries.
- **Cider vinegar** is made from apples, which give it a mild but tangy and fruity flavor. Use in pickles, coleslaw, or stir a spoonful into a glass of seltzer.
- **Malt vinegar** is made from unhopped beer or malted barley. A classic condiment with English "chips" (French fries), it may also be used in potato salad.
- **Rice vinegar** is made from white or brown rice, while rice wine vinegar is made from sake. Both are mild and almost sweet and good for low-fat dressings (because you need less oil to offset their flavor) or for dipping sauces.
- **Sherry vinegar** is made from sherry wine that has been aged in oak barrels. It's less sweet but just as complex as balsamic vinegar. Sherry vinegar makes a splash in soups like black bean, split pea, or gazpacho.
- **Wine vinegar** may be made from table wine or varietals like chardonnay and cabernet. White wine vinegars are milder than reds but both are fairly acidic. Sprinkle on steamed vegetables.

3.7 Meat, Dairy, and Egg Substitution Products

Meat analogues are made to simulate the taste and texture of meat and are helpful as transitional foods or as a mainstay for some vegan diets. Some are found in a refrigerator case, often in or near the produce section; others will be in a freezer case. A wide variety of different brands and styles are available:

- Sliced "deli" style – everything from sliced "bologna" to sliced "turkey"
- Hot dog and sausage style "meats" may be found in either the refrigerator or freezer.
- Veggie burgers are usually found in the freezer case.

Note: some varieties contain egg white or dairy products, so always check the ingredients list.

Milk alternatives, such as soy, almond, flax, hemp, rice, oat, and hazelnut milk, can often be found in the refrigerated case as well as in aseptic shelf-stable packages in the grocery section. Unsweetened, low-fat, and flavored (such as chocolate or vanilla) versions are also often available. Read the label to check for low-fat and low-sugar choices.

Cheese alternatives may be completely plant-based, or some may contain casein (milk protein) but are free of lactose and other dairy ingredients. Read the ingredient label to check. They can be soy, almond, rice, or other plant-food based, and are available in a variety of flavors and styles such as cream cheese and mozzarella. Many cheese alternatives now melt just like a dairy-based cheese when heated.

Nutritional yeast, found in the grocery section or in a bulk bin, is a dry powder that offers a cheese-like flavor. It comes in two sizes: maxi flake and mini flake. Maxi flake can be sprinkled on foods such as popcorn. Use mini flake when baking or in sauces. Note: despite its name, nutritional yeast will not function to make baked goods rise.

Yogurts (nondairy) may be made from soy, almond, coconut, or rice milk, in a variety of flavors. Look for those with minimal sugar or sweetener added, as many yogurts are highly sweetened. Unsweetened varieties are also available for those who prefer to add their own flavorings. See page 15 for information about probiotics.

Egg substitutes depend on how you would have used the eggs. For baking, bananas, applesauce, or ground flaxseeds can work well when combined with baking soda to encourage rising. Look for vegan cake recipes to learn how this is done. Egg Replacer, a packaged product, is a convenient alternative. For egg salad, mash tofu with vegan mayonnaise and spices, or try a packaged egg salad substitute, sold in containers available in the refrigerated case of many natural food stores. To make a dish like scrambled eggs, tofu is best mixed with spices following a recipe or using a premixed flavoring packet.

3.8 Healthy Alternatives

We recommend that you choose organic foods where available, and try to choose foods that are high in fiber and low in fat, sugar, and salt (*HiFi LoFaSS*). Here is a quick substitution chart to help you make healthier choices for a simple burger or a PB&J sandwich.

Instead of:	Much better choices:
A regular burger: • Hamburger • Cheese (dairy-based) • Mayonnaise • Ketchup • Iceberg lettuce • White-bread bun	A better burger: • Veggie patty (frozen, HiFi LoFaSS) • Vegan cheese • Vegan mayonnaise • Fresh tomato slices or low-sugar tomato sauce • Romaine lettuce, spinach • Whole-grain bun
A regular PB&J Sandwich: • Processed peanut butter • Strawberry jelly (high sugar) • White bread	A better PB&J Sandwich: • Unsalted, natural peanut butter • Apple sauce or natural fruit spread (no sugar added) • Whole-grain bread

CHAPTER 4

— BEFORE YOU GO SHOPPING —

4.1 Plan Your Menus

The best way to avoid wasting time and money is to plan ahead. Choose some recipes to make in the next week. Plan to buy all the ingredients you'll need for a week's worth of meals. Include food for breakfast, lunch, snacks, and dinner, but allow for the meals you'll most likely eat outside of the home. If you tend to cook in quantity, you may be able to make some meals from leftovers. Some people like to prepare all their meals for a week on one day, and then freeze them in portions ready to defrost as needed.

To find a good selection of recipes, buy a good vegan cookbook, such as *The Veg-Feasting Cookbook* by Vegetarians of Washington. The website www.nutritionmd.org is particularly useful for planning menus. If you set up an account, you can select healthy recipes for all of your meals, and it will help create an ingredient list for you.

If planning all your meals ahead of time doesn't work well for you, and you like to cook recipes as you feel inspired, you can also stock your kitchen with foods for recipes you make regularly. Be sure to always have a good selection of whole grains, canned beans, tomatoes, and other shelf-stable items available, plus frozen fruits and vegetables, convenience foods, and bread in your freezer. Then keep those basics replenished as you use them up, and buy only the quantities of fresh fruits and vegetables and other perishable items you expect to use right away.

Any method of organizing your food is acceptable. The trick is to find a method that works for your lifestyle so that you won't find yourself dashing to the store every day or ordering up junk food in desperation!

4.2 Make a List

Once you have a plan, check to see which ingredients you already have at home, and then make a list of all the items and quantities you'll need. A bewildering assortment of products is available in the stores, and it's easy to forget some of the items you needed to buy. Having a list will help avoid making extra trips to the store, saving both time and money.

Stores often carry smaller quantities of natural foods, since they have a shorter shelf life and limited shelf space, so sometimes you may find that your store is out of a product you need. For staple items, plan to replenish your supplies well before you run out so that you don't need to panic if you find that the store has run out.

4.3 Plan for Food Storage

Make sure you have the space in your kitchen cabinets, refrigerator, and freezer to store the food you're going to purchase. Most produce will keep longest by storing it in the refrigerator unwashed and in a plastic bag, although some people like to wash produce, especially fruit, as soon as they get it home so that it's ready to grab and eat when needed. Mushrooms keep better in a paper bag. Bananas and any fruit that needs to ripen should be stored in a fruit bowl, and other fruit may be kept in the fruit bowl in small quantities to encourage family members to choose fruit instead of less healthy choices for a snack! Nuts and oils also last longest when stored in the refrigerator.

Use your planned shopping trip as an incentive to throw away any food that is past the use-by date or that you don't think you'll use, especially from the refrigerator. If you have unopened nonperishable food items that you don't expect to use, give them to your local food bank, which will accept food even if it's past the sell-by date. Purchase rectangular-shaped, clear food containers to store bulk items such as whole grains and dried legumes—they're much easier to organize on shelves than bulky packages.

4.4 Gather Coupons

Coupons are among the best ways to save money. Find coupons for the products you intend to buy or the stores you prefer to use. Don't buy a product you don't typically use just to save money, but if it's a product you've been thinking of trying for the first time, a coupon can be helpful to get you started. You can get coupons from:

- Manufacturers' websites
- Coupon distribution websites
- The stores themselves

4.5 Grab Your Reusable Sacks

While the food you choose is far more important for the environment than the bag you use, reusable bags still help the environment. It can also save you money in those towns that have a bag fee.

4.6 Prevent Food Spoilage While Shopping

Did you know that if your refrigerated food is allowed to increase in temperature by only ten degrees, the number of potentially harmful bacteria will increase dramatically?

Always plan to purchase the most perishable items last, particularly those from the refrigerated or frozen case, especially if you have a lot of shopping to do. Take them straight home after purchasing them. In warm weather or when you have a distance to travel, you can also bring an insulated bag or place a cooler in your car with an icepack. Ensure that frozen and refrigerated items are separated at the checkout so that you can easily place them in the cooler. When you get home, unpack the perishable items first and get them into your fridge or freezer right away. That way you'll minimize the time the perishable items spend outside the refrigerator or freezer, and thus minimize the growth of harmful bacteria.

CHAPTER 5

— UNDERSTANDING FOOD LABELS —

It is important to read food labels carefully for many reasons: to check for unhealthy, allergic or animal ingredients, to compare the healthfulness of different brands, and to look for information about whether the food was produced ethically.

This information is best gathered from the Nutrition Facts and the Ingredients list, plus some certification labels. Most of the remaining information on a package is put there just for marketing purposes.

5.1 Tips for Label Reading

Date Marking
The Use By or Best Used Before date gives the date by which the food should be eaten. Avoid buying food past its Sell By date unless you will use it right away.

USE BY

BRAND NAME

BRAND NAME

SOY MILK

SOY MILK

Ingredients:
Soya beans, water, natural flavorings.

Nutrition Facts

KEEP REFRIDGERATED
Once opened please consume within 3 days

Manufactured By:
[Manufacturer's name and address here.]

300ml

Product Name
Usually beside the brand name. Tells you what the food is.

Ingredient List
This shows all the ingredients that make up the product. The ingredients are listed in descending order by weight.

Nutrition Information
This panel shows the nutrients found in one serving or in 100 g/100 ml of the food.

Usage Instructions
These are instructions for storing or using the product.

Manufacturer's Details
Every label includes the name and address of the manufacturer, importer, or distributor.

Net Weight or Volume
This gives the actual weight or volume of the food. For canned foods packed in liquid, the net weight is the weight of the drained food.

Start Here!
Compare your portion to the recommended serving size. For example, if your serving size is two cups, you will be eating double the calories and nutrients.

Limit These Nutrients
They raise the risk of the development of certain common diseases.

Quick Guide to % Daily Value
• 5% or less is low
• 20% or more is high

This label shows that a serving of the food provides 11% of the daily recommended amount of fiber. This means that you need another 89% to meet the recommended goal. These are estimates and apply if you are following a 2,000 calorie diet.

Check Calories
Check the total calories and calories from fat per serving.

Get Enough of These Nutrients
They help prevent chronic disease.

Nutrition Facts

Serving Size: 1 cup (28g)
Servings Per Container: 14

Amount Per Serving

Calories	100
Calories from Fat	15

	% Daily Value*
Total Fat 2g	3%
Saturated Fat 0g	0%
Polyunsaturated Fat 0.5g	
Monounsaturated Fat 0.5g	
Cholesterol 0mg	0%
Sodium 190mg	8%
Potassium 170mg	5%
Total Carbohydrate 20g	7%
Dietary Fiber 3g	11%
Soluble Fiber 1g	
Sugars 1g	
Other Carbohydrate 16g	
Protein 3g	

	% Daily Value
Vitamin A	10%
Vitamin C	10%
Calcium	10%
Iron	45%
Vitamin D	10%
Thiamin	25%
Riboflavin	25%
Niacin	25%
Vitamin B6	25%
Folic Acid	50%
Vitamin B12	25%
Phosphorus	10%
Magnesium	10%
Zinc	25%
Copper	2%

*Percentage Daily Values are based on a 2,000 calorie diet. Your daily values might be higher or lower depending on your calorie needs.

Label Reading Definitions

Phrase	What it means
Sodium:	
• Sodium-free or salt-free	Less than 5 mg per serving
• Very low sodium	35 mg or less of sodium per serving
• Low sodium	140 mg or less of sodium per serving
• Reduced or less sodium	At least 25% less sodium than the regular version
• Light in sodium	50% less sodium than the regular version
• Unsalted or no salt added	No salt added to the product during processing (this is not a sodium-free food)
Fat:	
• Fat-free	Less than 0.5 g per serving
• Low saturated fat	1 g or less per serving and 15% or less of calories from saturated fat
• Low-fat	3 g or less per serving
• Reduced fat	At least 25% less fat than the regular version
• Light in fat	Half the fat compared to the regular version
• Trans fat-free	Less than 0.5 g per serving
Fiber	
• High Fiber	At least 5 g fiber per serving

5.2 Certification Labels

What does "fair trade" mean?

Fair trade certification aims to help improve trading conditions for producers in developing countries, especially when trading with developed countries. It advocates the payment of a higher price to exporters as well as higher social and environmental standards, thus promoting sustainability. Fair trade certification also encourages better treatment for workers.

Some products that may be labeled "fair trade" include coffee, cocoa, sugar, tea, bananas, honey, cotton, wine, and chocolate, among others.

What does "gluten-free" mean?

Gluten is a protein found in wheat, barley, rye, and spelt. In addition, oats are often contaminated with gluten during processing. People with celiac disease need to completely avoid this protein. Others who have only a sensitivity to gluten may be able to tolerate small amounts. While there had been no regulation for products using the label "gluten-free" in the past, this has now changed. According to the FDA, a product may claim to be "gluten-free" if it meets the following criteria: it may not contain any gluten-containing grain, an ingredient derived from a gluten-containing grain (unless the gluten has been removed), or any ingredient regardless of source that contains more than twenty parts per million (a miniscule amount) of gluten.

What does the irradiated label mean?

Many foods, especially spices, are irradiated with either x-rays or the more powerful gamma rays in order to kill any disease-causing bacteria and increase shelf life in a cost-effective manner. The FDA considers the practice safe and effective, and there is no radiation risk whatsoever to the consumer. However, some people feel that  the chemical composition of the food may be changed in ways that may be undesirable. All irradiated foods are labeled with the symbol shown here. One way to avoid buying irradiated food is to simply buy organic.

What does "kosher" mean?

Kosher is the set of Jewish regulations regarding what foods can and cannot be eaten, how those foods can be combined, and how they must be prepared and eaten. However, many people other than the Jewish community, and some Christian groups who also keep kosher, rely on the kosher symbols to help select their food. In fact, according to studies by Mintel, an organization that analyzes food industry sales and trends, 21 percent of the American public now specifically looks for a kosher designation. The kosher market in America is now estimated to be $17 billion and growing by 10 percent per year.[4] Some 125,000 different kosher products are currently sold in America's supermarkets and grocery stores. The reasons for choosing kosher are varied: 55 percent of kosher consumers feel the products are healthier and safer, 38 percent are vegetarians looking for assurance of ingredients and integrity

4 Lariss Faw, "Is Kosher the Next Big Food Trend?" *Forbes*, December 2, 013, http://www.forbes.com/sites/larissafaw/2013/12/02/is-kosher-the-next-big-food-trend/

of processing, 35 percent feel that the taste and quality is higher, and 16 percent are following halal—a set of regulations for Muslims that are similar in some respects.[5]

Kosher symbols, such as those shown above, indicate that the food is kosher and that its entire production has been supervised by the koshering authority that uses the symbol on the package. The supervision is usually very strict: the ingredients and the equipment are inspected to protect against even minute amounts of contamination, and the cleanliness of the facility is carefully controlled and often must be witnessed on site.

Briefly, the regulations are as follows: certain animals may not be eaten at all, including pigs, insects, reptiles, many species of birds and fish, and all shellfish such as shrimp, lobster, and clams. This restriction includes the flesh, organs, eggs, milk, and all by-products of the forbidden animals. Very important is the regulation that milk cannot be mixed with mammal meat in any way, including on production equipment. This means that all food is put into the following categories: forbidden, neutral (can be used with either dairy or meat), dairy, or meat. Forbidden foods can't be certified kosher. Therefore you may encounter kosher symbols with an M for approved mammal meat, D for approved dairy, or P for pareve (neutral).

Plant-based consumers can look to avoid the D symbol to ensure that there are no dairy or dairy-derived ingredients in their food. Please note that even if there are no dairy ingredients, a designation of D will still be given if the equipment used was shared with dairy products. Consumers can be assured that there are no insect-derived ingredients such as carmine (often used as a coloring agent). Plant-based shoppers can also look for the kosher label on products such as parchment paper used in baking (where animal ingredients are sometimes used) or for supplements (where gelatin is often used instead of cellulose to make the capsules).

What does "organic" mean?

Organic foods are foods that are produced using methods of organic farming, which do not involve modern synthetic inputs such as synthetic pesticides and chemical fertilizers. Organic foods are also not processed

---

5 "Kosher Industry Facts," Kosher Fest, accessed June 9, 2015, http://www.kosherfest.com/kosher-facts

using radiation, industrial solvents, or chemical food additives. If you wish to avoid genetically modified ingredients (GMOs), buying 100% Organic, Certified Organic, and USDA Organic-labeled products is one of the easiest ways to do that.

According to the USDA's Agricultural Marketing Service, three different levels of organic foods are defined. The label "100% organic" indicates that the product is made only with certified organic ingredients and methods. If a product is made with at least 95 percent organic ingredients, it may be labeled "organic." The USDA Organic seal may be displayed on products that fit either of these categories. Products containing a minimum of 70 percent organic ingredients cannot display the USDA Organic seal, but the words "made with organic ingredients" can be used. The logo of the approving organic certification body may be displayed on all organic products.

Not everyone goes through the rigorous process of becoming certified, especially smaller farming operations. When shopping at a farmers' market, for example, don't hesitate to ask the vendors how their food was grown. Small manufacturers may simply say pesticide- and herbicide-free.

We recommend buying organic foods whenever they are available and affordable. They are better for both you and the planet.

What does the Whole Grain Stamp mean?

Grains such as wheat can be processed to a greater or lesser degree. In general, the less a grain is processed, the more nutrients and fiber it contains, so whole grains are nutritionally much better for you than refined grains. Many baked items, including bread and cookies, may include some whole grains to give their product the appearance of being healthier. However, they often still use refined grains for the most part, so it's important to read the ingredient list to see how much is listed as whole grain. If the first ingredient is not whole grain, the product is not as nutritious as it could be. The Whole Grain Stamp indicates whether the product contains some whole grains or whether the grains are 100 percent whole grains. While not all products use the stamp, when used they give an assurance that whole grains are used, since only companies that are members of the Whole Grains Council and submit information to the Council about their products can use the stamp on their products.

What does "GMO-free" mean?

GMOs (genetically modified organisms) are foods where one or more genes from one organism are spliced into the genetic structure of another. This is usually done in order to produce some desired effect, such as resistance to insects,  pests, or destructive molds and weeds. It is also used to boost the level of certain nutrients. Some people worry about GMOs since they feel that they haven't been sufficiently tested for any harm before being approved for sale as food.

"GMO-free" means that there are no GMOs used in the production of a food item. At present, the only available label is a verification seal from the Non-GMO Project. Their website states that verification is an assurance that a product has been produced according to consensus-based best practices for GMO avoidance. They are not able to certify that a product is totally GMO-free, since factors beyond a producer's control, such as pollen drift and contamination, can occur. Organic standards similarly require best practices to avoid use of GMOs, so anything that is certified organic is also GMO-free, so far as is possible. Keep abreast of pending state regulations for any further developments on GMO standards and regulations.

5.3 Understanding Ingredient Lists

The ingredient list on food packaging is a very important source of information, since you can use this list to determine how processed a food item is and whether it contains any ingredients you are looking to avoid. While fresh produce has no ingredient list, every prepackaged item should have an ingredient list, with ingredients listed in descending order of weight.

- Choose natural ingredients over artificial chemicals, artificial flavors and colors, preservatives, and stabilizers, if possible.
- Compare brands of packaged foods carefully, and choose foods that are high in fiber and low in fat (oils and fats, especially saturated and partially-hydrogenated ones), sugar (including sucrose, dextrose, fructose, high-fructose corn syrup, etc.), and salt (*HiFi LoFaSS*).
- Avoid animal-based ingredients.
- If you are purchasing food from a store's deli section, make sure to ask the clerk to check the ingredients on all prepared food to make sure it's as *HiFi LoFaSS* as possible and free of animal products.

Animal Ingredients to Keep an Eye Out For:

While most animal ingredients are obvious from their name, there are some ingredients that you may not realize are derived from animals. You may wish to avoid these ingredients:

Food

- **Albumen** – egg protein
- **Carmine or Cochineal** – a food-coloring agent used for its red color, derived from an insect
- **Casein** – milk protein
- **Gelatin** – derived from animal hooves
- **Keratin** – animal-derived coating agent
- **Lactose** – milk sugar from dairy sources

- **Lanolin** – oil from sheep's wool
- **Magnesium Stearate** – used as a coating and may be either plant or animal derived; the label usually indicates which
- **Renin or Rennet** – coagulant used in dairy industry but derived from cow stomachs
- **Whey** – protein from dairy

Health and Beauty Aids

Look for "Not Tested on Animals," "Cruelty Free," "Leaping Bunny" certification, or a PETA symbol, and avoid the following ingredients where possible:

- **Allantoin** – used in shampoos and creams; animal derived
- **Gelatin Capsules** – animal derived. Look for V caps alternative, which are derived from plants.
- **Vitamin D3** – may be from animal livers or from wool oil. Look for Vitamin D2, which is plant derived and just as effective.

For more information on ingredients and whether they are derived from animal products, the Vegetarian Resource Group has a comprehensive guide to food ingredients available online at www.vrg.org/ingredients.

Gluten Ingredients

While most people do just fine with gluten, some people have significant health problems with it. For those who wish to avoid gluten altogether, look for a gluten-free label (see page 49). For those looking to minimize gluten, the following is a list of ingredients to watch out for (source: *Gluten-Free Diet: A Comprehensive Resource Guide* by Shelley Case):

- Barley (flakes, flour, pearl)
- Breading, bread stuffing
- Brewer's yeast
- Bulgur
- Durum (type of wheat)

- Farro/faro (also known as spelt or dinkel)
- Graham flour
- Hydrolyzed wheat protein
- Kamut (type of wheat)
- Malt, malt extract, malt syrup, malt flavoring
- Malt vinegar
- Matzo, matzo meal
- Modified wheat starch
- Oatmeal, oat bran, oat flour, whole oats (unless they are from pure, uncontaminated oats)
- Rye bread and flour
- Seitan (a meat-like food derived from wheat gluten, used in many vegetarian dishes)
- Semolina
- Spelt (type of wheat also known as farro, faro, or dinkel)
- Triticale
- Wheat bran
- Wheat flour
- Wheat germ
- Wheat starch

These other ingredients may be less familiar to you, but they also contain gluten:

- Atta (chapati flour)
- Einkorn (type of wheat)
- Emmer (type of wheat)
- Farina
- Fu (a dried gluten product made from wheat and used in some Asian dishes)

MSG (Monosodium Glutamate)

MSG is used as a flavor enhancer, making certain flavors more fully experienced or intense. At one time MSG was mostly found in Asian foods, but nowadays it's widely used in almost all cuisines and many different products.

While most people don't seem to have any problems with MSG, and the FDA considers it safe, some people report having reactions to MSG such as headaches, flushing, and tingling. Some of those who are sensitive will only react to large amounts of MSG, but some can react to even small amounts.

For those who are sensitive to MSG, label reading is critical. According to the FDA, foods containing added MSG list it in the ingredient panel on the packaging as monosodium glutamate. However, MSG also occurs naturally in ingredients such as hydrolyzed vegetable protein (not to be confused with textured vegetable protein), autolyzed yeast, and hydrolyzed yeast. Foods with any ingredient that naturally contains MSG cannot claim "No MSG" or "No added MSG" on their packaging. MSG can also not be listed as "flavoring" or "spices."

Both soy sauce and tamari naturally contain small levels of MSG. For those wishing to use soy sauce, low-sodium tamari would be a better choice in order to reduce MSG exposure as much as possible. Bragg Liquid Aminos is another option for those who wish to reduce but not completely eliminate MSG.

Please note that despite some similarity in name, glutamate contains no wheat gluten.

Commonly Used Natural Food Additives

There are so many food additives used these days that it is impossible to name them all. However, there are two classes of additives made from natural ingredients that are very common, and it's worth explaining what these are and how they are used.

Sugar Alcohols

Don't be confused. Although they share a similar name, sugar alcohol and alcoholic beverages do not have the same chemical structure. Sugar alcohol does not contain ethanol, which is found in alcoholic beverages.

Sugar alcohols are used as sugar alternatives. They are naturally found in various fruits and vegetables. Commonly used sugar alcohols include sorbitol, xylitol, isomalt, and erythritol. They are not as sweet as sugar, so more needs to be used to achieve the same sweetness in recipes.

These sweeteners have the advantage of having less calories and not promoting tooth decay. Diabetics often find that sugar alcohols help manage their blood glucose better than sugar. The disadvantage is that when consumed in larger quantities, they can cause bloating and flatulence, and have a laxative effect. One exception to this is erythritol, which makes it the preferred choice.

Sugar alcohols are widely used in a large variety of foods as well as in products such as mouthwashes and toothpaste. You'll find the amount used in packaged foods listed in the nutrition panel under the sugar listing. They are also sold separately in some bulk bins as well as on the shelf.

Thickeners, Texturizers, and Emulsifiers

Not to be confused with chewing gum, food gums are used to give thickness and body to drinks and also to make pudding-like gels. They can also make for a smoother texture in a wide variety of foods. You can find them as an ingredient in packaged food or sold separately for use in the kitchen. As with all food, be sure to check the expiration date.

Agar-agar, alginate, and carrageenan are made from seaweeds. Xanthan gum is a fermentation product made by beneficial bacteria. Cassia gum, carboxymethyl, cellulose, cellulose gum, gellan gum, guar gum, hydroxypropyl cellulose, konjac, locust bean gum, methylcellulose, microcrystalline cellulose, and pectin are all made from different plants and specialty crops.

Lecithin can be an invaluable culinary ingredient. It is often present in vegan or low-fat cooking as an alternative to fat in baked goods, and it improves moisture and texture at the same time. It's also commonly used as an emulsifier to prevent separation in a wide variety of foods such as nut butters and chocolate. It also gives food a smoother texture by acting as a lubricant.

CHAPTER 6

IN THE STORE

Grocery stores are usually divided into sections, such as fresh produce, grocery items, frozen items, refrigerated items, and non-food items such as household items, pet food, health and beauty products, etc.

6.1 Fresh Produce Section

Most grocery stores import food from around the world to ensure a continual supply of fresh produce year round, but fresh produce ages the farther it has to travel, making it less fresh and often more expensive when it's out of season locally, so buy local produce in season whenever possible. Try to eat with the seasons, but for produce you need when it's not in season, frozen is often a good alternative. Frozen food is packed at its best so the goodness is frozen in.

Superstar produce items are those that have the best nutrients for your health, compared with similar common ingredients you might typically use. Examples are blueberries, pears, broccoli, kale, collard greens, sweet potatoes, tomatoes, and mushrooms. Try to avoid the classic iceberg lettuce, which has very little nutritional value. Romaine, red leaf lettuce, and spinach have much better nutritional profiles.

Selecting good fresh produce is important for food to look appetizing, taste good, and avoid spoilage and waste, although selecting less

than perfect produce can sometimes save quite a bit of money. Most produce is best bought as firm, crisp, and free of blemishes as possible, but it depends on if you want to use them immediately or store them for a while. You will learn by experience to recognize how ripe some items are and whether they'll work for the way you plan to use them. Most stores allow you to select your own produce, but some may prepackage the produce, which limits your choices. Here are some hints on how to select some of the most common items:

- **Apples** – Look for firm, crisp apples with as few bruises (flat areas on the surface indicates a bruise) as possible. Get to know the different varieties. Red apples tend to be the sweetest.
- **Avocados** – Very firm avocados will usually ripen in a few days. To use immediately, choose avocados that yield to the touch without being overly soft.
- **Bananas** – Green bananas usually ripen to yellow in a few days. Spotted bananas are sweetest, but once they're mostly brown, they are overripe and can only be used in smoothies or baking.
- **Berries** – Buy only when in season (or buy frozen), and look for any signs of mold or mushiness.
- **Broccoli** – Look for a crisp feel and dark green color. Yellowing indicates that it's past its best.
- **Carrots** – Fresh, whole carrots should be orange and firm, not limp. Peeled baby carrots are very convenient. Bags usually include water to keep them fresh. They should not be dried out or slimy.
- **Cauliflower** – Look for the head to be as white as possible. Yellowing indicates that it's past its best.
- **Citrus fruit** – Look for a firm texture and a vibrant color. Avoid bruising or wrinkles.
- **Corn** – Buying with the husk keeps corn ears fresh longer. Look for a bright-green husk.
- **Green beans** – Look for crisp green beans that snap in half easily.
- **Greens** – Look for crisp greens that are not limp or tarnished at the edges. Prepackaged salad greens are very convenient.
- **Melon** – A heavy feel and the smell of melon is the best indicator of ripeness.

- **Mushrooms** – Look for firm texture that has not dried out. Brown patches indicate that they are past their best.
- **Peaches** and other soft fruit – Look for a soft feel, without any mushy patches.
- **Pears** – Look for pears that yield to the touch. Like bananas, a few blemishes are fine. Really firm pears will ripen in a few days.
- **Peppers** – Look for firm, unwrinkled, and unblemished peppers.
- **Pineapple** – Look for a yellow color rather than green. You should be able to smell a ripe pineapple.
- **Potatoes** – Most blemishes can be cut off during preparation, but a green patch or sprouting is a sign that they have been exposed to too much light. Green potatoes should be avoided.
- **Tomatoes** – Ripe tomatoes should yield to the touch, but the skin should not break. Avoid wrinkles.
- **Watermelon** – Look for the patch where the melon sat on the ground. It should be yellow rather than white, if it has ripened on the vine. Tapping the melon and feeling the vibrations can help indicate whether it's overly ripe. Alternatively, ask the produce staff to cut it for you, and buy just a piece.

Produce is categorized as certified organic (grown without pesticides, herbicides, fungicides, GMOs), pesticide-free (often transitional farms that have not sprayed but haven't yet had the time for residues to degrade from their soil), or conventional. The Environmental Working Group has put together lists of produce that are the highest in pesticides (the Dirty Dozen), and those which typically have the lowest levels of pesticides found on them (the Clean Fifteen), in the United States. If you can't afford to buy all organic produce, consider choosing organic versions when buying items in the Dirty Dozen list. Conventional produce at lower risk of pesticide exposure can be selected from the Clean Fifteen list. For the latest list, see www.ewg.org/foodnews/.

2015 Dirty Dozen™ Plus

1. Apples
2. Peaches
3. Nectarines
4. Strawberries
5. Grapes
6. Celery
7. Spinach
8. Sweet bell peppers
9. Cucumbers
10. Cherry tomatoes
11. Snap peas
12. Potatoes
13. Hot peppers
14. Kale/Collard greens

2015 Clean Fifteen™

1. Avocados
2. Sweet corn
3. Pineapple
4. Cabbage
5. Sweet peas
6. Onions
7. Asparagus
8. Mangos
9. Papayas
10. Kiwi
11. Eggplant
12. Grapefruit
13. Cantaloupe
14. Cauliflower
15. Sweet potatoes

6.2 Grocery Shelves

Snack food doesn't have to be junk food. Snack foods are very convenient when you're traveling or when you don't have time for a meal. With careful reading of the ingredient list and food labels, it is possible to find snack foods that are on the healthier side. Check out the upper and lower shelves, as they often contain better bargains than at eye level and are also where new products may be found.

- **Dried fruit** – While fresh fruit is best, dried fruit is extremely convenient and tasty. Look for pure fruit with no added oils. While the natural sugars can be very concentrated, the fiber makes this a good snack food.
- **Snack bars** – Choose bars that have more grams of fiber than sugar or fat. Read the ingredients to ensure there are no dairy products.
- **Chocolate bars** and treats are usually high in sugar and fat, often containing milk or milk fat. Find products with dark chocolate (cocoa butter only) for the occasional sweet treat. Some chocolates have stevia as a sweetener instead of sugar.
- **Chips** – Look for baked or low-fat chips that are low in sodium and high in fiber. There are many kinds of chips these days made from various vegetables or beans. These chips often have more fiber than regular potato chips.
- **Popcorn** – Popcorn is very healthy, but many prepackaged varieties contain added fat, trans fat, salt, and dairy-based flavors, so be sure to check the ingredients. Air-popped popcorn is best, and you can sprinkle a little nutritional yeast on it to make it delicious.
- **Soda** – Water, tea, and coffee are great drinks on a regular basis, but if you're in the mood for soda, look for natural sodas sweetened with stevia or luo han guo (monk fruit extract). Alternatively, try seltzers flavored with fruit essences. These are naturally calorie-free and quite refreshing.

Useful food items found in the grocery section include whole grains and cereals such as wheat, barley, quinoa, oats, and rice; beans such as lentils, garbanzos, and black beans (dried or in cans); tomatoes (canned, sauce, or concentrate); soups and vegetable stock; shelf-stable nondairy milks; nuts such as walnuts and brazil nuts; seeds such as pumpkin and sunflower seeds; oils and vinegars; herbs and spices; and specialty foods.

In stores where bulk bins are available, learn how to use them. Usually you measure out the amount you want into a plastic bag, and then write a bin number on the twist tie to help identify the item at the checkout. Bulk bins are a great way to save money by buying only the amount you need, and to cut down on packaging and its environmental footprint. Nutritional information is usually printed on the bins themselves, so read the labels carefully or bring a memo pad to make notes. It's useful to have storage containers ready at home to store your bulk bin food items in the kitchen.

6.3 Frozen Foods

More and more food is finding its way to the frozen section these days. Frozen food often keeps for a long time and is a good choice when you might not eat the item in question until sometime in the future. Frozen fruits and vegetables are particularly useful if you like to make smoothies, find that fresh produce often goes bad before you can use it, or for when fresh produce is out of season. However, home freezer space is often limited, so don't buy more than you can fit.

In addition to frozen fruits and vegetables, there are usually many prepared food items in the freezer case. While it's best to prepare as many meals as you can from basic ingredients, some of these prepared foods can be great time-savers for a quick meal, especially veggie burgers, burritos, and complete meals. However, it is still important to read the food labels to avoid animal ingredients and to choose foods that are *HiFi LoFaSS* as possible.

HiFi LoFaSS = High in fiber; low in fat, sugar and salt.

6.4 Refrigerated Foods

This is where you may find products such as tofu, tempeh, and meat or dairy alternatives, although in some stores they may be found in a separate natural food section. See page 38 for more information about these. Buy these items last, as they are the most vulnerable to spoilage. Make sure to note the expiration dates before you buy, and don't buy more than you have space for in your home refrigerator.

6.5 Deli Section

Many large grocery stores have a special deli section, where pre-pared salads, soups, sandwiches, and even whole meals may be available to purchase and eat right away. Many of these are not very "veg-friendly" at present, but natural food stores often have good plant-based options in their deli. If you don't see what you want in the deli section, be sure to ask. While they may not have the food you want today, if enough people ask for something, you may soon find that they start offering it.

6.6 Natural Food Section

Some stores have a natural foods section where they gather more natural packaged, refrigerated, and frozen foods together, especial-ly plant-based items. These can be useful to help find healthier natural foods quickly. Other stores have mainstreamed those veggie burgers right in with the conventional burgers. Some stores may do some of each, so if you don't see what you're looking for in a natural section, check out the main aisles where you might still find it, or ask for assistance.

6.7 Special Orders

If you don't see what you want, ask the store to special order an item for you to pick up at the store when ready. There's no need to be shy about this! Today's grocery stores and supermarkets are happy to do it and are usually set up for it. Ordering through the stores has some advantages over using the Internet alternatives:

- No shipping charges – This is especially valuable for heavy or bulky items.
- No worrying about receiving deliveries or having them left on your doorstep.

- No worrying about frozen and refrigerated items, since the stores will keep them in their cold storage.

If you're looking for a product they are unable to order for you, consider looking online. Some good websites for online food ordering include:

- www.healthy-eating.com
- www.veganessentials.com
- www.veganstore.com

Afterword

With a little menu and recipe planning ahead of time, and careful attention to food labels and ingredient lists in the store, it is easy to purchase a good selection of plant-based foods at a reasonable cost. It may take you extra time on your first few visits to the grocery store, but once you become familiar with where food items are located in your favorite store, and you recognize the packaging of the brands with high quality ingredients, you'll become a super-shopper in no time.

Further Resources

For information about why to go vegetarian or how to switch to a plant-based diet, here are a few resources that we recommend:

Websites:

- **Vegetarians of Washington (www.vegofwa.org)** – Vegetarians of Washington is a leading nonprofit vegetarian society based in the state of Washington. It has a free e-newsletter (The Vegetarian Page), an informational site for doctors (The Vegetarian Prescription), and a mobile app that can be downloaded for Apple and Android devices.
- **NutritionMD (www.nutritionmd.org)** is a website that offers plant-based meal plans, nutritional advice, and a huge supply of recipes.
- **Vegetarian Times (www.vegetariantimes.com)** – The Vegetarian Times magazine maintains a huge database of vegetarian and vegan recipes, plus weekly e-newsletters.

Books:

- *Say No to Meat: The 411 on Ditching Meat and Going Veg* **by Amanda Strombom and Stewart Rose** – Find the answers to all your questions about going vegetarian, including practical and social issues. Included is a selection of easy recipes to get you started.
- *The Vegetarian Solution* **by Stewart Rose** – This is a comprehensive look at the many benefits of a vegetarian diet. Written in a lighthearted and supportive style, this book provides detailed information on how a vegetarian diet can improve your health and the world you live in.
- *The Veg-Feasting Cookbook* **by Vegetarians of Washington** – This cookbook offers a delicious range of recipes from the best vegetarian and veg-friendly restaurants and local chefs in the Pacific Northwest. Covering a full range of cuisines, this cookbook includes all the recipes you'll ever need.

- *Eat Vegan on $4 a Day* by **Ellen Jaffe Jones** – If you're shopping on a budget or are under the misimpression that it's too expensive to go veg, then this book is for you. With tips and hints for keeping the costs down, and money-saving recipes, this book comes highly recommended.

About the Authors

Stewart Rose

Stewart is the vice president of Vegetarians of Washington and has been following a vegan diet for about thirty-five years. He enjoys teaching people about the many benefits of a vegetarian diet: for their health, for the environment, and for all the living things who share the world with us. Originally from New York City, he lives in the Pacific Northwest with his wife, Susan, who is also a longtime vegan.

Amanda Strombom

Originally from England, Amanda has lived in the United States since 1997. A vegetarian for over twenty years, and more recently a vegan, she loves to teach people how to shop for and cook plant foods. She is the president of Vegetarians of Washington and recently became a certified Food for Life instructor. She lives in the Seattle area with her husband, Doug, where they have raised two vegetarian children.

Vegetarians of Washington

Something special is happening in the Pacific Northwest. Formed in 2001 and based in Seattle, Vegetarians of Washington quickly grew to be one of the largest, if not the largest, vegetarian societies in the country. While Vegetarians of Washington provides community and events for the vegetarians and vegans in the region, the organization places particular emphasis on helping the mainstream public discover the benefits and experience the pleasures of a vegetarian diet, comprised of fruits, vegetables, whole grains, legumes, and nuts.

Monthly catered dinners, classes on why and how to go veg, talks to interested groups, and information booths at fairs and festivals form the basis of the organization's year-round activities. Over the years, Vegetarians of Washington has written several books to help people learn about the benefits of this way of eating, and to discover new recipes to cook and restaurants where they can enjoy delicious vegetarian meals. See page 69 for more details.

Seattle Vegfest is the highlight of the year, and possibly the largest vegetarian food festival in the United States. This healthy and delicious vegetarian food festival, held at the Seattle Center in the spring of each year, brings together the whole vegetarian community to showcase to the mainstream public the many types of vegetarian food available. Medical doctors give informational talks on how people can improve their health with a plant-based diet, nonprofits explain the benefits to the environment and all living things, chefs and cookbook authors demonstrate how to cook vegetarian food, clowns play with the kids, and best of all, samples of over five hundred different kinds of food are available to try.

The Prescribe Vegetarian Campaign is the latest and most ambitious project of Vegetarians of Washington. The goal of the campaign is to change the medical school curriculum so that it teaches students how to use plant-based diets to prevent and treat many diseases. The campaign also reaches out to practicing physicians and provides them with education on plant-based diets that they can use to benefit their patients.

Vegetarians of Washington is a warm and friendly organization where people are encouraged, while making changes to their diet, to proceed at their own pace and just do the best they can. You don't have to be a vegetarian or vegan to come to any events, or even to join the organization. To learn more, or to join, visit www.VegofWA.org.